MW00997762

SMELLING AND TASTING

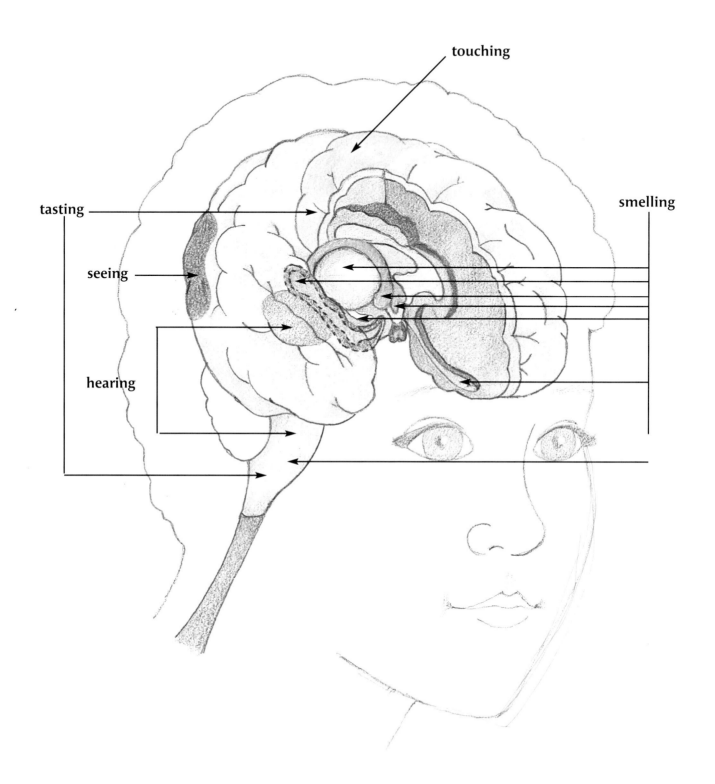

touching

smelling

tasting

seeing

hearing

SMELLING AND TASTING

Dr. Alvin Silverstein, Virginia Silverstein, and Laura Silverstein Nunn

Senses and Sensors
Twenty-First Century Books
Brookfield, Connecticut

Cover illustration by Anne Canevari Green

Photographs courtesy of PhotoEdit: pp. 8 (© David Young-Wolff), 10 (© David Young-Wolff), 13 (© David Young-Wolff), 53 (© James Shaffer); Animals Animals/Earth Scenes: pp. 15 (© J. Mitchell/OSF), 38 (© Fabio Colombini), 40 (© Hamman/Heldring), 42 (© Carol J. Kaelson), 43 (© Austin J. Stevens), 44 (© Donald Specker), 49 (© Deni Bown/OSF); Photo Researchers, Inc.: pp. 16 (© Stuart Westmorland), 27 (© Professor P. Motta/Department of Anatomy/University La Sapienza, Rome/SPL), 51 (© Geoff Tompkinson/SPL), 55 (© Geoff Tompkinson/SPL), 57 (© Geoff Tompkinson/SPL); Visuals Unlimited: pp. 17 (© Joe McDonald), 19 (© Bill Beatty); Omni-Photo: pp. 29 (© Grace Davies), 47 (© Laura Dwight)

Illustrations by Anne Canevari Green

Library of Congress Cataloging-in-Publication Data
Silverstein, Alvin
Smelling and tasting / by Alvin Silverstein, Virginia Silverstein, and Laura Silverstein Nunn
p. cm — (Senses and sensors)
Includes bibliographical references and index.
ISBN 0-7613-1667-1 (lib. bdg.)
1. Smell—Juvenile literature. 2. Taste—Juvenile literature. [1. Smell. 2. Taste. 3. Nose. 4. Tongue.
5. Senses and Sensation.] I. Silverstein, Virginia B. II. Nunn, Laura Silverstein. III. Title. IV. Series.
QP455 .S48 2001 612.8´6—dc21 2001018089

Published by Twenty-First Century Books
A Division of The Millbrook Press, Inc.
2 Old New Milford Road
Brookfield, Connecticut 06804
www.millbrookpress.com

Copyright © 2002 by Dr. Alvin Silverstein, Virginia Silverstein,
and Laura Silverstein Nunn
All rights reserved
Printed in the United States of America
1 3 5 4 2

Contents

SMELLING AND TASTING

Do you relish the smell of freshly baked cookies? Perhaps you've enjoyed tasting them in the past? The senses of smell and taste have a very important relationship to each other and to how we relate to our environment.

One
THE FORGOTTEN SENSES

Smell those chocolate chip cookies baking in the oven! Your mouth starts to water, and you can almost taste the cookies melting in your mouth. Do you like the sweet-smelling fragrance of a bouquet of roses? What about the smell of hot popcorn or peanuts at a carnival? Do these kinds of smells and tasty foods make you think about some good times you've had?

Some other smells and foods may not be so pleasant. You can probably tell when something is burning on the stove by the smell of smoke in the air. A carton of milk that smells funny lets you know that the milk will taste sour and you should not drink it. And a stinky piece of bread with fuzzy green stuff growing on it is a sure sign not to eat it. You could never forget the unpleasant odor given off by a skunk. That kind of smell makes you want to run away—fast!

Researchers have used our sense organs as models to develop artificial devices that are even more effective. For example, electronic "noses" can sniff out tiny differences in foods and other things. These devices can not only identify chicken that is spoiling but even tell how many days the chicken was stored and whether it was kept in the refrigerator the whole time or allowed to warm up. Other electronic noses can detect buried land mines by sniffing the odors of tiny amounts of explosive chemicals that escape into the air or help to diagnose diseases by sniffing a sick person's breath.

DID YOU KNOW?

The senses of smell and taste are often linked to one another. These two senses work together when we appreciate the flavors of foods.

9

Have you ever thought about how useful your sense of smell is in your daily life? Many people don't realize that they are using their sense of smell unless a scent is intense or extremely unpleasant.

Living Sensors

All living organisms—humans, animals, and even plants—have senses. Everything we know about the world comes through our five main senses—sight, hearing, smell, taste, and touch. In this book, we will discuss the senses of smell and taste, their relationships, and their importance in helping us to learn about the world around us. Whether we are smelling flowers or spoiled milk, tasting sugar cookies or raw onions, our minds receive impressions of the world. The messages from the nose, mouth, and other sense organs are interpreted by the brain and turned into meaningful information.

The sense organs gather information about the world through specialized structures called **sensors**. These sensors detect various types of energy and send information about them to the brain. Some animals have sensors that far exceed our own. Dogs are famous for their superior smelling abilities. A dog's nose is millions of times more sensitive than a human's. A shark can hunt down its prey underwater with its keen sense of smell. A catfish has fifty times more taste sensors than the average person does.

Chemical Sensors

Both smell and taste are chemical senses. The specialized sensors in your nose and mouth detect bits of the chemicals that make up foods and other things in our world. Researchers have also invented devices to detect chemicals in the air or water. These artificial sensors can be very effective in picking up even tiny traces of particular odors or tastes. Some artificial noses and tongues change color when they detect a particular chemical; others include a tiny computer chip that identifies odor chemicals by comparing the electrical changes they produce with a set of standards. These devices actually translate chemical sense messages into visual messages—numbers or patterns that people see with their eyes.

We tend to rely mainly on our vision and hearing, major senses that help to connect us with the outside world. We take the senses of smell and taste for granted. Most people do not pay attention to smells and tastes unless they are unusually intense, pleasant, or unpleasant. But we are born with the ability to develop all of our senses to the fullest. If we can learn to become more attuned to our "forgotten" chemical senses, we can discover a whole new world that we did not realize was there.

Two
THE Chemical Senses

Did you know that everything in the world is made of chemicals? The air you breathe, the water you drink, the food you eat, the house you live in, and even your own body are all made up of various chemicals, combined in various ways. The basic building blocks of each kind of chemical are called **molecules**. They are so small that you cannot see each individual one, even with a magnifying glass; more powerful techniques are needed to look at the molecules that make up the things in our world.

Chemicals in Our World

Some chemicals are solid, like those in a book or a table or the sidewalk. Normally, they don't change their shape or size. Other chemicals are liquids, such as those in water or milk or gasoline. They normally stay the same size but can easily change their shape, as you can see if you pour water from a tall, thin bottle into a short, wide glass. Still other chemicals are gases, such as the oxygen and nitrogen in the air you breathe. You can't see the gas molecules in air, but you can feel them if you blow on your hand.

If they are heated, chemicals may change their state from a solid into a liquid (like a melting ice cube) or from a liquid into a gas. (You can see the wisps of steam coming off the top of a pot of boiling water as some of its molecules pass from the liquid to the gaseous state.) Even in a solid, some of the molecules may escape into a gas form and bounce off into the air. Scientists say that chemicals that tend to turn into gases fairly easily are **volatile**. The

Some of the chemicals in flowers are very volatile. If you sniff them, they give off a strong and distinctive scent.

wood of a tabletop is not very volatile, but if you put your nose close to it and sniff, you will find that it has a distinct "woody" odor. Your nose is picking up molecules of some of the volatile oils and other chemicals from the wood and its protective coating. The chemicals in perfumes are very volatile, and so are many of the chemicals in foods.

In addition to escaping into the air by turning into gases, some of the chemicals in foods and other things can **dissolve** in liquids such as water or alcohol. If you drop a sugar cube into a glass of water, it will gradually get smaller until it seems to disappear. But you can tell that the sugar is still there by tasting the water. It tastes sweet. The individual sugar molecules have dissolved, spreading out evenly through every part of the water in the glass. Warming the glass or stirring the water can help the sugar to dissolve faster.

Chemical Detectors

Living organisms have special sensors called **chemoreceptors**, which detect chemicals that come into contact with them. When contact with a chemical activates the chemoreceptors, they send messages along sensory nerves to the brain, which interprets the signals into meaningful information. Animals use this information to locate food, find a mate, communicate, and avoid danger. Some plants take advantage of animals' chemical senses, producing sweet-smelling chemicals to attract insects that carry pollen from flower to flower, or bad-smelling and bad-tasting chemicals to chase away animals that might eat them.

Animals that live on land and breathe air have two separate chemical senses: smell (**olfaction**) and taste (**gustation**). The chemoreceptors in the organs of smell pick up volatile molecules in the air, while the sensors in the organs of taste respond to chemicals dissolved in water. But for fish and other animals that live in the water, the distinction between the chemical senses is not as clear-cut. A shark picks up "smells" in water with sensors very much like the chemoreceptors in your nose, and it processes and uses the information these sensors provide in much the same way land animals perceive odors drifting in the air currents.

Tiny single-celled creatures such as the amoebas and paramecia that live in ponds detect chemicals in the water directly, because their entire body surface is surrounded by water. But more complex, multicelled organisms need specialized equipment for detecting and analyzing chemicals. Among animals, from tiny mosquitoes to enormous elephants, the chemical sense organs vary a great deal.

Animal Smell Sensors

Most animals have some sort of structure that can detect smells. These structures contain special cells called **olfactory receptors**, which make smelling possible. The receptors are so sensitive that they can pick up even the slightest hint of specific molecules in the air or water. Many animals depend on their sense of smell for survival.

The simplest form of chemical detection can be found in **invertebrates**, animals without backbones. (The "skeleton" that supports their body structures is the outer covering of the body.) The moth, for instance, does not smell through a nose, like the one we have. It has two feathery-looking antennae, which contain highly sensitive olfactory receptors that can detect odor molecules at great distances.

Moths' antennae have such sensitive olfactory receptors that they use them to locate food, communicate with each other, and even find a mate.

Other insects, including mosquitoes, ants, bees, and wasps, also have smell-detecting structures on their antennae, tiny hairs that can detect odor molecules in the air. You have probably noticed how mosquitoes tend to be attracted to chemicals in human skin, particularly sweat. Fortunately, mosquitoes do not like certain odors such as eucalyptus, citronella, lavender, and cinnamon. You can buy products that contain these scents to ward off these pests.

A shark's sense of smell is so remarkable that it can locate a single drop of blood in 25 gallons (95 liters) of water—the amount it takes to fill a wading pool. A shark can pick up the scent of its prey from about a quarter of a mile (400 meters) away.

Animals that have smelling structures similar to those of humans can be found among the **vertebrates** (animals with a backbone and internal skeleton). The sense of smell in this group of animals is a bit more complicated than what we have seen among the invertebrates.

Sharks are the champion scent detectors of the ocean waters. A shark smells through two openings, called **nostrils**, located on the underside of the snout. It does not breathe through its nostrils as we do. Sharks use their nostrils for only one purpose—to find food. In fact, the sense of smell is so important that an estimated 70 percent of a shark's brain is devoted to smelling. Inside a shark's nostrils are nasal sacks, which contain chemical-sensitive membranes necessary for smelling. As water rushes into the nostrils, chemicals in the water trigger the olfactory receptors located on the membranes, which then send signals to the brain for processing.

A salmon will leave its home in the ocean and travel as many as 1,000 miles (1,600 kilometers) back upstream to its birthplace in the river to lay its eggs. And it can do this just by following its nose! The salmon's nose consists of two small openings, called **olfactory pits**, connected by U-shaped tubes. As the salmon swims, water flows through one opening and then out the other. The scent chemicals in the water activate the olfactory receptors, which then send messages to the salmon's brain. Scientists have found that salmon can find their way home because they had learned to recognize the smell of their home waters when they were just baby fish.

A snake flicks its tongue in and out to pick up scent molecules in the air and bring them into its mouth where the olfactory receptors are located.

Many lizards and snakes smell with a special structure called the **Jacobson's organ**. It is found in the animal's mouth, not its nose. You have probably seen a snake flick its tongue in and out. It almost looks as if it is trying to sting you with its long, forked tongue. But what it is actually doing is picking up scent molecules in the air with its tongue and bringing them into its mouth. The tips of the forked tongue are brought into the Jacobson's organ, which is located in two small pockets in the roof of the snake's mouth. The Jacobson's organ contains olfactory receptors, which collect information about the snake's surroundings. When the sensory cells are activated, messages are sent to the snake's brain and interpreted.

Super Sniffers

The human nose contains six to ten million olfactory receptors. But that's not nearly as impressive as the dog's nose, which contains 150 to 220 million receptors. Some dog breeds, such as German shepherds and bloodhounds, which help police sniff out illegal substances or track down criminals, are reported to have up to a billion receptors! These super sniffers have helped people in many other ways as well. Dogs have been used to locate egg masses laid by gypsy moths, chemicals used by arsonists to start fires, explosives, guns, land mines, leaks in gas lines, and termite nests in houses. They have also helped to rescue victims in avalanches and earthquakes and to search for missing children.

Once the snake identifies the smell, it can take action, whether to strike at a potential meal or to beware of danger.

Turkey vultures can do something most other birds can't—find food by smell. Vultures are scavengers, which means that they eat dead animals. A good sense of smell is very helpful in locating rotting flesh. But the turkey vulture's relatives, the North American black vulture, the American condor, and the California condor, have a very poor sense of smell. So they follow turkey vultures around during their hunting flights. When a turkey vulture finds food, its greedy cousins try to steal its meal.

While humans see the world with their eyes, a dog "sees" the world with its nose. A dog's nose is so sensitive that most of its brain is devoted to identifying smells. Dogs can detect some odors that are millions of times too faint for people to smell.

Animal Taste Sensors

Most animals have some sort of structure that can detect tastes. These structures contain sensitive cells called **gustatory receptors**. The sense of taste usually involves direct contact with the substance.

Taste gives important information about food. When the taste receptors are activated, they send messages to the brain. If the food is acceptable, the animal can eat. But if the brain interprets the food as poisonous or bad tasting, the animal will reject it.

The simplest taste receptors can be found among the invertebrates. Many insects, including bees, butterflies, and flies, get their first taste through the tips of their feet or **tarsi**. The tarsi have tiny hairs that contain taste receptors. A bee can taste with many different parts of its body—its tongue, nose, antennae, feet, and knees! Many insects are drawn to sweet tastes. Bees are famous for their love of sweet nectar. Bees and flowers have the perfect partnership. Flowers provide the bees with a supply of sweet nectar, and bees help to pollinate the flowers during feeding.

Crustaceans, including shrimp, crabs, and lobsters, actually use the same sense organs to smell and taste. Their chemoreceptors are tiny hairs located on their legs, mouth, and antennae. The sensitive hairs pick up chemicals from a distance. This is how the animal smells potential food. When food is in close contact, the

DID YOU KNOW?

Parrots are the best tasters in the bird family. Unlike many other birds, they have taste receptors on their tongue.

*Many butterflies enjoy the taste of sweet nectar. They unroll their long coiled beak, called a **proboscis**, to explore a flower. The proboscis is used like a straw to suck up the nectar.*

The Taste Race

The catfish has more taste receptors than any other animal. As many as 175,000 taste receptors give it super-tasting abilities. The animals with the worst sense of taste are chickens. They have only twenty-four taste receptors! So they don't have much need for variety when it comes to food.

animal tastes the food with the hairs on its legs and mouth.

Many of the catfish's taste receptors are located on the outside of its body—so it can actually taste the food before it eats it. For a catfish, taste is its most important sense. It travels through very cloudy and murky waters, and its vision is not very good. So the catfish uses its sense of taste to find its way. Taste receptors in its **barbels** (whiskers) help to locate its food. The barbels move around from side to side, almost like radar, trying to detect food.

Frogs and toads have taste receptors in a more familiar place—in their mouth. These amphibians, like many other vertebrates, taste with tiny taste receptors grouped into structures called **taste buds**. The frog uses its long, sticky tongue to snap up insects at a distance, so tasting is an important part of this animal's life. A frog's taste buds are similar to those of a human but are located on the underpart of the tongue. (Humans' taste buds are on the upper surface of the tongue and in the back and roof of the mouth.) But the frog can taste better when the tongue is outside its mouth than rolled up inside. That's because the frog's taste buds are spread out over a larger area when it stretches its tongue out to catch its food.

Snakes are among the few vertebrates that don't have any taste buds. The snake's tongue cannot taste anything at all. But it knows when something is good to eat through its sense of smell, as mentioned earlier. Just by taking chemicals in from the air, it can sense if a good meal is nearby.

Most birds have a poor sense of taste. Their taste buds are found in their mouth and throat, but none on the tongue. Birds that feed on seeds on a sandy ground may not know if what they are eating is tasty. Birds that feed on nectar or fruits have a more developed sense of taste.

Three
HOW WE SMELL AND TASTE

What would you do if you couldn't smell or taste? How would you feel about a pizza if you could not smell its aroma or taste the blend of cheese, tomato, spices, and fresh-baked crust? It would be like eating wet cardboard.

We actually need both senses of smell and taste in order to experience flavor. Try holding your nose and eating some food. How did it taste? Did it seem bland? It probably did. The same thing happens when you eat food while you have a cold and your nose is stuffed up. Foods don't seem to have as much taste as usual. That's because when we eat, air is brought upward from the mouth while we are chewing. The nose is connected to the mouth and throat, so what we consider to be "taste" is largely due to our sense of smell.

Our sense of smell does more than just give food flavor. It also acts as a warning so that we won't eat things that can make us sick. For instance, the odor of spoiled milk or rotten eggs is a sure sign that we should not put these things in our mouth.

Inside the Nose

The nose is our organ for smelling. Noses come in all shapes and sizes, but they all do the same job—detect scent chemicals in the air. When you breathe in air, the chemicals enter your nostrils, the two openings in your nose. Once inside the nose, the air flows through two tunnels called **nasal passages**, which lead up into the **nasal cavities**. On the roof of each nasal cavity is a mucus-covered patch called the **olfactory epithelium**. It is only the size of a

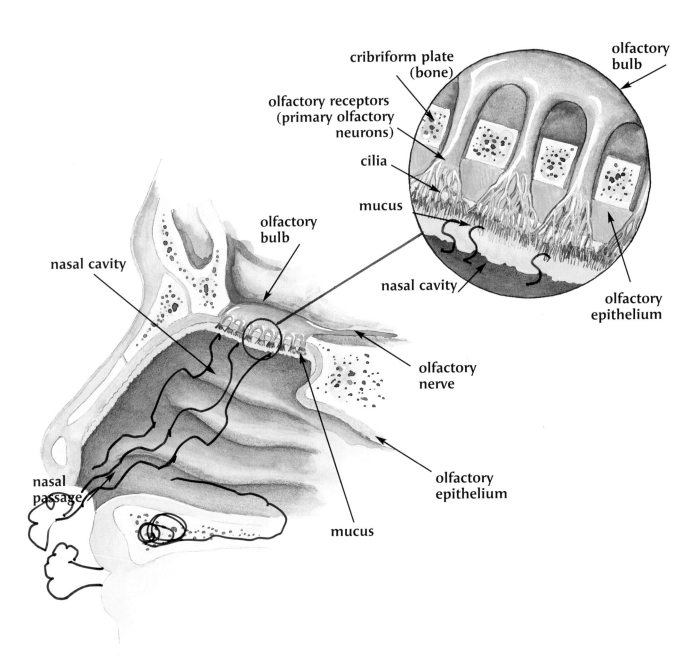

cribriform plate (bone)

olfactory receptors (primary olfactory neurons)

cilia

mucus

nasal cavity

olfactory epithelium

olfactory bulb

nasal cavity

olfactory bulb

olfactory nerve

olfactory epithelium

nasal passage

mucus

postage stamp, but it contains millions of olfactory receptors. Each receptor-filled patch ends in a knob, from which six to twelve tiny olfactory hairs, or **cilia**, dangle into the gooey mucus. The olfactory receptors are stimulated when odor molecules are dissolved in the mucus and picked up by the dangling cilia. Researchers have found that there are from five hundred to one thousand different kinds of odor receptors in the nose of a rat or mouse. They believe humans may have a similar number.

The thousands of tiny **nerve fibers** (long, thin branches of **neurons**, cells that are specialized for carrying messages) from the olfactory cells are gathered into a rope of fibers called the **olfactory nerve**. Messages from the olfactory nerve are carried to the brain. Unlike the other senses, the sense of smell has a direct connection to the brain. The olfactory receptor cells are actually nerve fibers. They run straight through to the brain.

Special areas of the brain are devoted to receiving and analyzing messages sent from the nose. The brain then makes sense out of the information from the nose and turns it into something we can understand—a fragrant flower, a stinky skunk odor, or smelly sneakers.

The delicate cells that carry olfactory receptors are in a very exposed position, protected from the outside world by just a coating of mucus. These cells are continually getting damaged, and they gradually accumulate a load of old odor chemicals. Fortunately, unlike most other nerve cells, the olfactory receptors can be readily replaced. The old, worn-out cells, with their loads of chemicals, are discarded like bags of garbage and are flushed away with the mucus. New cells move out to take their place. The new olfactory cells first form deep within the membrane lining the nasal cavity. As they move to the surface, they sprout olfactory cilia. Typically, the lifetime of an olfactory receptor cell is about four to five weeks.

To stimulate an olfactory receptor cell, an odor chemical must have three main characteristics. It must be volatile, to get into the air that is drawn into the nose. It must be able to dissolve in water, so that it can pass into the mucus coating. It must also be soluble in fats, so that it can penetrate into the fatty covering of the receptor cell.

What's That Smell?

Some scientists believe that there are a number of basic types of receptors, each of which responds to a specific type of odor. Researchers suggest that different kinds of smells have particular molecular shapes. The body's smell receptors are designed to fit these various shapes, like a key into a lock. If an odor molecule stimulates only one type of receptor, then we smell only that smell, but if other receptors are stimulated as well, there is a blend of odors.

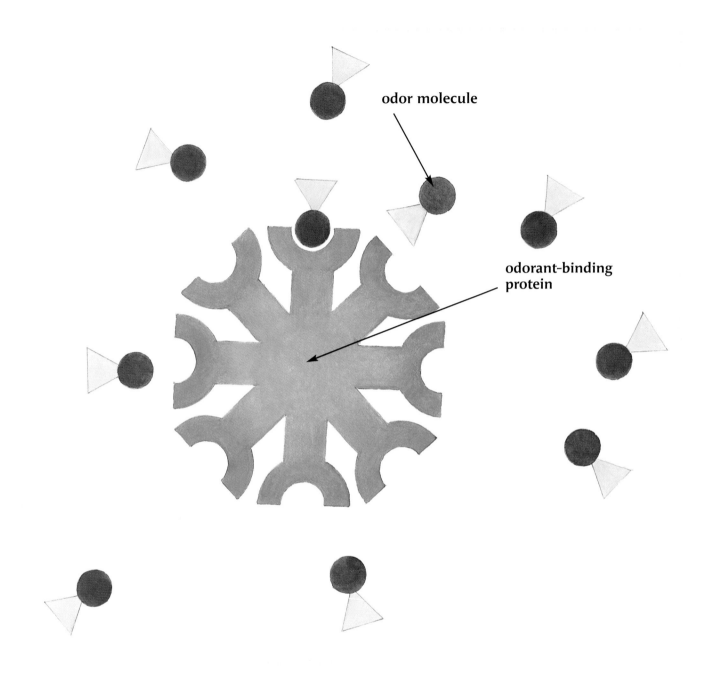

odor molecule

odorant-binding
protein

Odor molecules fit right into the cup-shaped openings of the odorant-binding protein, which carries odor molecules from the air up through the mucus to the olfactory cells.

Researchers working with rats have discovered that a tiny duct at the tip of the rat's nose continually sprays a fine mist into the inhaled air. This mist contains proteins that bind to odor molecules. These **odorant-binding proteins** (OBPs) have cup-shaped openings into which the odor molecules fit. The OBPs carry odor molecules up through the mucus to the olfactory cells. They help to concentrate the odor molecules from the air, bringing similar ones together, so that even very tiny amounts of odor chemicals can be detected. The researchers believe that humans' sense of smell also involves such OBPs.

For centuries, scientists have been trying to classify odors. One classification suggests seven primary groups of odors: musky, floral, pepperminty, ether-like, camphoraceous, pungent, and putrid. Other suggested systems include nine categories, and one modern smell researcher believes there are more than thirty different primary odors. The thousands of distinct odors that we can recognize are the result of various combinations of the primary odors.

Smelling in Stereo

Researchers have found that people's nostrils take turns: One of them is always slightly swollen, but every few hours they switch roles; the nasal passage that was swollen clears up and the other one swells. Now Stanford scientists report that the differences in airflow (you breathe in less air through the swollen nostril) make tiny differences in the way the sensors in the nasal lining respond to odor chemicals.

The slightly different messages these sensors send to the brain help to improve our ability to distinguish among the odors we smell.

Smell Fatigue

Have you ever noticed that the delicious odors you smell when you first walk into a bakery seem to fade away as you wait in line? Or perhaps you have visited a public rest room that hasn't been cleaned often enough. The smell seems disgusting at first, but by the time you leave you don't notice the bad smell as much.

These effects are examples of olfactory or smell fatigue. When a smell particle reaches a receptor cell on the olfactory membrane, it fills up a spot. If the smell is strong, soon all the receptors that respond to that particular odor are filled. Those receptor cells have already sent their smell messages to the brain. They will not be able to send out any more signals until the odor chemicals have been disposed of. So we become adapted to the smell.

Born With Taste

Although we can learn to like certain foods, the variations in the sense of taste are inherited. That's why foods can taste differently to different people. The link between taste and heredity has been demonstrated in studies. A chemical known as PTC (phenylthiocarbamide) is often used to test taste heredity. For most people, PTC is a bitter-tasting substance. But between 15 and 30 percent of the population cannot taste PTC. The tendency to be a PTC "taster" or "nontaster" is hereditary.

Different smells have different detection thresholds—that is, different numbers of particles need to be present before a person will notice the smell. If we breathe in a whiff of pine cleaner first, for example, the smell of baking chocolate chip cookies might not be as strong—or as good—as usual. That's how "deodorizers" work. They do not really remove the odors in a room; instead, they send out an odor of their own that overwhelms the smell receptors, producing a sort of jamming effect. We therefore don't smell the other odors in the room.

Our Taste Sensors

We taste with our tongue. If you look at your tongue in the mirror, you'll notice that it has a rough, pebbly texture. The surface of the tongue is covered with tiny bumps called **papillae**. Under a high-powered microscope, you would see that these little bumps contain the taste receptors—your taste buds. Each papilla contains a cluster of taste buds, which look like tiny flower buds or cabbage heads, surrounded by finger-like projections. Inside the buds are **taste receptors**, which are sensitive to chemicals. The taste buds react to chemicals that dissolve in the **saliva**. Saliva is the watery fluid in your mouth that is released by the salivary glands. It is essential in the tasting, chewing, and swallowing of food. Most of the taste buds are found on the surface of the tongue, but they may also be in the throat, the cheek, and the roof of the mouth.

When food chemicals come into contact with the taste buds, receptors on the taste cells are stimulated and send impulses to a branching network of taste nerve fibers, interwoven among the taste cells. These impulses are then relayed along other nerves to special areas in the brain for processing. There are no special "taste nerves" that connect directly with the brain, corresponding to the olfactory nerves that carry smell sensations. Instead, taste messages

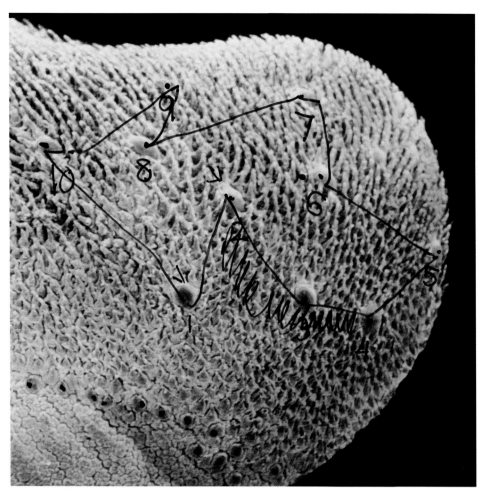

This image of the tongue's surface seen through an electron microscope shows the papillae, which contain our taste receptors.

travel along parts of several different nerves that pick up touch and other sensory messages from the face and throat.

What's That Taste?

Humans can eat a wide variety of foods. Some foods taste better than others, but this preference varies from person to person and even in the same person at different times. Did you ever find that you were developing a liking for a food that you used to think tasted yucky? We can often learn to develop a taste for certain foods.

Taste Buds for Life

Babies are not born with all of their taste buds. You probably don't have all of yours yet, either; you will be adding more as you grow. Adults have about ten thousand taste buds. Like other cells in the body's coverings, taste cells and the taste buds that contain them continually wear out and die. They are replaced by new ones every ten days or so. But as people grow older, the body's repair processes get less efficient. Some of the taste buds that die are not replaced. By old age, a person may have as few as three thousand taste buds left. Older people find they can't taste things as sharply as they used to. Favorite foods may suddenly begin to taste unpleasant. But recent studies have found that older people tend to like certain vegetables better than they used to because they have lost some of the taste buds sensitive to bitter tastes.

There are four main kinds of taste buds. Each kind responds to a particular taste—sweet, sour, salty, and bitter. Taste buds are not found all over the tongue, but only in certain parts of it. Taste buds of the same kind are grouped together. Those for sweet tastes are at the front of the tongue. Taste buds for salt are at the sides toward the front. Those for sour tastes are farther back on the sides, and the taste buds for bitter tastes are spread across the back of the tongue. Most taste buds are sensitive mainly to just one of the primary tastes, but they may also respond to others to some degree.

Even though there are only four kinds of taste buds, we can taste hundreds of different flavors. How is this possible? The flavors of most foods are actually blends of the four primary tastes, just as many different shades of color can be blended from the primary colors red, yellow, and blue. Because the four kinds of taste buds are found on different parts of the tongue, sometimes we can taste two or more distinct flavors in the same food. You can see how this is possible if you have ever had sweet and sour pork, a Chinese dish. You can taste both sweet and sour flavors at the same time.

Actually, our perception of flavors is more complicated than this. A large part of what we think of as "taste" is actually contributed by our sense of smell. When you bite into an apple or chew a piece of steak, volatile chemicals from the food enter your nose and produce smell sensations that blend with the taste of the food in your mouth. When you have a cold, food seems tasteless because your nose is too stuffed to allow you to smell.

People generally find sweet tastes pleasant and bitter tastes unpleasant. These reactions are part of the body's automatic warning system: sweet foods in reasonable amounts are usually good and wholesome, while many poisons have a bitter taste. Sour and salty tastes are pleasant in small amounts but unpleasant in large amounts. So "bad" tastes, in a sense, act as a warning of danger, sending your brain a message to stay away from certain foods that may be harmful.

Researchers have recently discovered that people vary greatly in their sensitivity to strong tastes. Tests with a bitter chemical called PROP (6-n-propylthiouracil) show that it tastes rather bitter to about half the population; about a quarter find it so bitter that they may throw up, and a quarter can't taste it at all. The people who react violently to PROP—"supertasters"—have a large number of papillae on the surface of the tongue, containing a large number of taste pores that allow chemicals to enter. The medium tasters have fewer papillae and taste

Try This Taste Test

Start with an assortment of different-flavored hard candies, such as Lifesavers. Close your eyes and hold your nose. Now have someone hand you one of the candies, without telling you what flavor it is. Put it in your mouth while still holding your nose. What do you taste? You may get a clear impression of a sweet or sour taste, but does the candy have a cherry or grape or lemon flavor? Now let go of your nose and breathe naturally while you suck on the candy. Most people can't tell what flavor the candy has until they open their noses and can breathe in the odor chemicals that it gives off into the air.

The Fifth Taste

Recently, researchers have discovered a fifth kind of taste receptor, which responds to a chemical called glutamine, commonly found in foods, especially meats and ripe cheeses. We perceive the signals from the **glutamine receptors** on the surface of taste buds as a sort of meaty or savory taste. Scientists call it **umami,** from a Japanese word meaning "delicious savory taste." **Monosodium glutamate** (MSG) is a form of glutamine used as a seasoning in cooking. It is commonly found in Asian dishes but is also used in many other kinds of foods, such as pizza with a sausage topping. MSG helps to bring out the flavors of foods and make them tastier.

pores, and the nontasters have the smallest number of papillae, with far fewer pores. The supertasters also have strong reactions to the tastes of foods. They tend to avoid strong-tasting foods, such as broccoli, grapefruit juice, coffee, and hot peppers. They even dislike very sugary foods, although most people have a natural liking for sweet tastes—the icing on a cake is just too sweet for a supertaster, and the artificial sweetener saccharine has a strong aftertaste. They also avoid very fatty foods. (Fat does not have a particular taste, but fat molecules press against the taste buds, producing a sensation that the brain interprets as "greasy.") With those food preferences, it is not surprising that supertasters tend to be thinner than the average.

Four
THE BRAIN CONNECTION

Our smell and taste senses are so remarkable that we can close our eyes and easily distinguish between similar smells and foods with similar flavors. You can probably smell the difference between a pair of dirty gym socks and a skunk odor, or between a bouquet of flowers and a bottle of floral perfume. Our sense of taste is pretty discriminating too. Without looking, you can tell by the taste whether you have taken a bite out of an apple or a peach, or a pork chop or a steak.

Our nose and mouth are effective organs for sampling the chemicals in our world, but, alone, they cannot make sense of what we are smelling or tasting. The olfactory receptors in the nose carry messages directly to the brain, where they are analyzed and processed. The taste receptors in the mouth send information about the tastes to the brain for interpretation. Parts of the brain are devoted to analyzing messages about smells, and other areas are devoted to tastes. It is in these special places that we can distinguish between various smells and various tastes. For tastes, the brain also uses information about the odors that go with them.

Learning from Experience

A newborn baby's brain is not yet able to interpret all the messages from the sense receptors. It learns as it is presented with new experiences. When you smell an odor or taste a food or drink, your brain compares the new sensation to patterns from past experiences. You

DID YOU KNOW?

We can distinguish many more smells than tastes. We can also pick up much tinier amounts of odor chemicals than taste chemicals. It is estimated that the sense of smell is about ten thousand times more sensitive than the sense of taste.

can recognize the smell and taste of a cheese pizza because your brain remembers the smells and tastes of pizzas you ate in the past. You can even learn to distinguish pizzas made with different kinds of cheese or other toppings. Your memories of smells and tastes are especially sharp and strong if the past experience was notably pleasant or very unpleasant, and the sense memories will be closely linked with these past encounters. You will find the smell of cheese pizza appealing if your family served pizza at parties where you had a lot of fun, but that same smell would be upsetting if you got sick and threw up right after eating pizza for the first time. The strong link between emotions and the senses of smell and taste is part of the way these sense messages are processed in the brain.

Our Ancient Brain

In the history of animal life on Earth, the chemical senses were the first to develop. They provided a way to detect and seek out food sources. Later, animals began to use chemical senses to "sniff out" other important things, such as familiar territories, enemies, and potential mates. In our distant ancestors—fish, reptiles, and the early mammals—a substantial part of the brain was devoted to processing information from the chemical senses, particularly the sense of smell. Later, other parts of the brain expanded and became increasingly complex. In the human brain, only a small portion is devoted to receiving and processing smell and taste messages. The largest part of our brain is the **cerebrum**, the "thinking brain."

The Nose in Your Brain

Sense messages travel from the olfactory receptors into the brain. The first stop along the way is a bulb-shaped structure the size of a match head. This is the **olfactory bulb**, found in the lower part of the brain just above the nasal cavity. (The brain actually has two olfactory bulbs, one on each side, corresponding to the two nostrils of the nose.) To get to the olfactory bulb, a **primary olfactory neuron** (the nerve cell running up from the olfactory epithelium in the nose) must thread its way up through the bony skull that covers and protects the brain. It passes through a thin portion of the skull called the **cribriform plate**, which is pierced with holes like the top of a saltshaker.

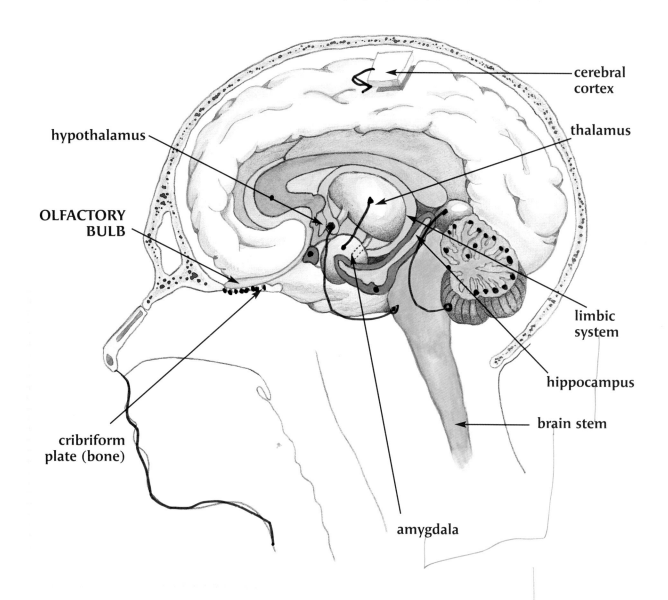

cerebral cortex

thalamus

hypothalamus

OLFACTORY BULB

limbic system

hippocampus

brain stem

cribriform plate (bone)

amygdala

There are about five million olfactory receptors in each side of the nasal cavity, and a primary olfactory neuron connects each one to the olfactory bulb on the corresponding side. Within the olfactory bulb, these olfactory neurons meet at nerve clusters called **glomeruli**. Researchers have found that the neurons corresponding to a particular kind of odor receptor all join at the same place in the olfactory bulb. They form a kind of map of the information provided by the different types of odor receptors. There are only a thousand or so glomeruli in each olfactory bulb. Each one sends

Smells and Memories

French writer Marcel Proust was flooded with memories when he smelled the aroma and tasted a piece of cake called a madeleine. It amazed Proust that the smell and taste of this little cake could evoke such powerful memories of long ago. Proust recorded all these memories in an eight-volume novel.

You can probably think of examples from your own experiences in which a particular smell brought back a vivid memory. But are memories associated with smell really stronger and longer-lasting than those linked with the other senses? Some experiments suggest that they are. In one study, for example, volunteers were exposed to a series of new smells and taught to recognize them. Retests a month later showed that the volunteers still remembered all the smells just as well as they had only a few minutes after learning them. In another study, people remembered up to 65 percent of a set of test smells a year after they had first been presented. But they had forgotten 50 percent of a comparable series of photographs after only four months.

messages into other areas of the brain, along secondary olfactory neurons. About twenty-five secondary neurons travel from each glomerulus up into the brain, to the specialized **olfactory areas** of the **cerebral cortex**, located at the sides of the head. In these areas, odors are identified by the particular combinations of nerve signals from the different types of receptors.

Most of the nerve cells that run through your body are surrounded by a fatty covering called a **myelin sheath**. Like the insulation around a telephone wire, the myelin sheath protects the nerve cell and helps messages to flow quickly and efficiently. But the olfactory neurons do not have a myelin sheath. The lack of a myelin sheath means that the nerve messages they carry travel more slowly, but it also permits more nerve cells to be packed into a smaller space—so they can carry more information to the brain.

Secondary olfactory neurons connect the olfactory bulbs to many parts of the brain. Some go to the **hypothalamus**, a structure deep inside the brain that contains centers controlling appetite, fear, anger, and pleasure. Other smell fibers loop down to the brain stem, where breathing and other automatic functions are controlled. Still others pass up into the cerebral cortex, the thin outer layer of the cerebrum that forms the "thinking brain." An olfactory area, specialized for interpreting sense messages relating to smell, is found at each side of the cerebrum. There are also close links with the parts of the brain that scientists call the **limbic system**, involved with emotions. These include the **thalamus** (a kind of central switchboard that sorts out and relays incoming information), the hypothalamus, parts of the cerebral cortex, and the **hippocampus** and **amygdala**, two structures involved in the formation of memories. This close linkage is the reason that odors can call up such strong and long-lasting memories of past experiences.

Messages from our other sense organs, such as the eyes and ears, are just "raw data," which are sorted out in specialized centers in the brain. All the thousands of colors we see, for example, are distinguished by the visual center in the brain on the basis of messages from just three types of receptors in the eyes—for red, green, and blue light. But the nose contains different kinds of receptors for each kind of odor chemical, so much of the information on smell is already sorted out before it ever reaches the brain. It is the brain, however, that makes all these different odors meaningful, linking them with experiences to form memories that help to guide future actions. The brain also decides which odors can bring pleasure and satisfaction, and which ones are warnings of danger.

The Tasting Brain

Unlike the olfactory and other senses, there is no single sensory nerve carrying taste messages into the brain. There are actually *three* gustatory nerves: the **lingual nerve**, a major nerve at the front of the tongue, the **glossopharyngeal nerve**, at the back of the tongue, and the **vagus nerve**, found at the throat and windpipe. These sensory nerves, which carry the taste sensations from the different parts of the mouth, come together in the bottom part of the brain stem, called the **medulla**. From here, they travel to a small cluster of cells in the front of the **brain stem**, the thalamus. Finally, the taste signals follow a pathway into a taste-receiving area in the cerebral cortex, where they are interpreted. Thus, we know what we are tasting.

The nerves that carry taste messages travel along with nerves carrying other sense messages from the tongue. The taste area in each side of the brain is located in the same part of the cortex that receives messages from tongue sensors that send information on touch and temperature. Actually, our perception of foods includes

DID YOU KNOW?

The "smell brain," consisting of the olfactory bulbs and the olfactory areas of the cerebral cortex, is called the **rhinencephalon**, from Greek words meaning "nose in the head."

not just their taste but also something food scientists call "mouth-feel"—the texture, thickness, and so forth. Smell sensations, processed in the olfactory areas, also make up a large part of what we think of as taste.

Certain things can affect our sense of taste. Foods at extreme temperatures (very hot or very cold), for instance, can temporarily turn off tasting mechanisms. The sense of taste works best when things are at or just below body temperature. Another factor that can affect taste is that after you hold something in your mouth for a while, you become less sensitive to that taste and also to other foods with a similar taste. As with the sense of smell, you become adapted to a taste after prolonged exposure. Tasting may also involve a contrast effect. For instance, studies have shown that water tastes sweet after you eat something sour. And it tastes salty after you have eaten something bitter.

Five
THE TALE CHEMICALS TELL

A worker ant's eyesight is not very good, but she has a keen sense of smell—enough to sniff out a tiny crumb of food on the ground. Tapping and probing the morsel with her feelers, she gets an idea of its shape and size, then picks it up and carries it back to the ant nest. The ant can pick up some pretty heavy objects, but sometimes, when pieces of food are too big for one ant to carry, she has to get some help. Hurrying back to the nest, the ant stops from time to time to touch the tip of her abdomen to the ground. Each time, she releases a tiny drop of chemical through her stinger. Back at the nest, the ant is met by others from the colony. Sniffing at the ant with their antennas, they soon show signs of excitement. Some of the ants rush outside, sniffing at the ground. Soon they pick up the traces of scent the returning ant had laid down. Before long, a line of ants leaves the nest along the odor trail to the food. When they reach it, they work together to chop it into smaller pieces and carry the pieces back to the nest.

Communicating By Smell

Not only ants but practically all animals that have a good sense of smell use odors as a kind of language. For these animals, chemicals are a major part of their lives—it's how they communicate within their species. Different scent chemicals and combinations of them carry a lot of information. They provide a complete personal identification and also communicate moods and feelings such as contentment or fear. Some animals will release special chemicals

Many animals, including ants, communicate with their superior sense of smell by giving off distinct scent chemicals to relay messages.

that warn others of approaching danger. Some animals transfer their personal smells to objects around them—like an identification label or a chemical *No Trespassing* sign. You have probably noticed neighborhood dogs out on a walk scent-marking trees, fireplugs, and other objects. Odors make convenient trail markers, and they also serve as a means of advertising. Female cats and some other mammals, for example, announce their readiness to mate using scent signals.

Chemicals that an animal produces and releases into its surroundings to communicate with others of its species are called **pheromones**. (*Phero-* comes from a Greek word meaning "to carry"; the ending, *-mones*, emphasizes the similarity to hormones, which are chemicals used for communication inside the body.) Some animals also produce smells to communicate with animals of other species; these are called **allomones**. (The prefix comes from a Greek word meaning "other.") The best-known allomone is the spray that a frightened skunk squirts out from special scent glands on its rear. Skunk spray contains sulfur compounds that are particularly strong and unpleasant-smelling. If a skunk is attacked, it douses the attacker with this smell and then quickly makes its escape. These predators usually learn to stay away from skunks in the future.

Chemical Mating Calls

Smell plays an important role in reproduction. A male moth, for example, has an amazing ability to find a mate several miles away just by following the female's scent. When the female is ready to mate, she produces a **sex attractant**, a kind of pheromone that helps male moths find her. The volatile chemical spreads through the air and is carried by the winds far and wide. Each tiny hair in the male's feathery antennae contains highly sensitive smell receptors that react to particular odors. Male silkworm moths, for example, respond to a chemical called bombykol, which is produced in the abdomen of female silkworm moths. A single molecule of bombykol in the air is enough to start a male silkworm moth searching for more of the odor. As he gets closer to the female that released the sex attractant, its concentration in the air increases. He keeps flying until he finds the female. (Actually he may also find some competition. Each female produces about ten-millionths of a milligram of bombykol, but this tiny amount would be enough to attract one billion males!)

Researchers have isolated the chemicals in sex attractants from various insect pests, such as gypsy moths, pink bollworms, and cockroaches. They have developed methods of synthesizing the pheromones artificially and have been testing them as lures for trapping and killing the pests.

Among mammals, smell also plays a very important part in finding and recognizing a mate. In most species, the female is able to mate only for brief periods of time. In some species, this receptive period occurs only once or twice a year; in others, the sexual cycle repeats every few days. When the female is ready to mate, she sends out sex pheromones. The male also has his own sex pheromones, which may help to make females receptive or to influence their choice of a mate.

Many mammals, including rodents, carnivores, and grazing animals use their **vomeronasal organ** (VNO) to respond to mating calls. The vomeronasal organ is a cigar-shaped structure located at the front of the nasal cavity. It is connected to the mouth by a duct in the roof of the mouth. The function of the VNO in mammals is similar to the Jacobson's organ in reptiles—they both collect and analyze odor molecules.

Mammals such as lions, horses, goats, and rhinos explore odors by lifting their upper lip and jaw to expose their vomeronasal organ, which collects and analyzes odor molecules.

The VNO is very sensitive to pheromones. You have seen the VNO at work if you have ever watched a cat sniff around and then lift its upper lip and jaw as it zeros in on a smell. This is called the **flehmen response**. It occurs when the animal is investigating the body odors and urine of another animal. By lifting its upper lip and jaw, the animal is exposing its VNO so it can zero in on the odors.

Humans also have a vomeronasal organ during early development in the mother's womb. But after a few months, the VNO shrinks. Some researchers believe that human adults still have a working VNO and that it is a very sensitive organ that responds to chemicals, such as skin secretions and artificial pheromones. These chemicals produce electrical signals in the cells of the VNO that cause mood changes in people. Interestingly, studies show that the sensitivity of the VNO to chemicals in skin secretions depends on the person's sex. For instance, the VNOs of male volunteers responded to a chemical found in women's skin, and the VNOs of female volunteers responded to one from men's skin. More recent studies, however, contradict the claims that humans have a functional VNO. Researchers have discovered that the gene responsible for response to pheromones is mutated and nonfunctional in humans.

The VNO in humans still remains a controversial topic. However, scientists agree that people produce body chemicals that could act as pheromones. This effect can be seen in women during their monthly menstrual cycle. Studies have shown that a group of women living in the same residence will eventually menstruate around the same time each month. The timing of their monthly cycles is reset by the chemicals secreted by their housemates.

Personal Identification

When you take a dog for a walk, expect the dog to stop frequently to sniff the ground wherever you go. Your dog is gathering information about the neighborhood creatures and their recent activities. Lingering smells reveal that a cat passed by or a squirrel scampered up a tree. But the dog is most interested in the smell news about other dogs in the area. Each one has left pheromone traces with every step, from scent glands in its paws. Other glands near its rear put scent markers on the dog's feces, and still other glands pour pheromones into its urine. Your dog, reading these odor traces, can tell exactly which dogs have passed by recently, their sex, age, and even their mood. Meanwhile, your dog is leaving its own contributions to the neighborhood "smell newsletter" when it deposits its own pile of feces or stops to squirt urine on a tree trunk or fire hydrant.

Many mammals use pheromones to mark trails or outline the boundaries of their home territory. Male cats "spray" a mixture of urine and scent chemicals on trees, bushes, and rocks to inform other cats of their presence. Cats also have scent glands on their

Bloodhounds are used to track scents for modern day law enforcement, as well as search and rescue, because of their superior sense of smell. Trained bloodhounds can follow a trail that is several hours old by detecting foot scents on the ground and body scents brushed off on plants.

cheeks and chin; they mark familiar objects (such as their human owners) by rubbing their faces against them. Lions and other wild cat relatives use scent markings in similar ways.

Newborn animals also respond to their mothers' particular scent. Newborn kittens, for instance, can find their way to their mother's nipples to nurse even though their eyes are sealed shut. In fact, each kitten in the litter soon settles down to its own personal nipple on its mother's belly. Researchers have discovered that the kitten finds its way to the milk supply and recognizes its assigned nipple by smell.

Mammal mothers and babies of many species use their sense of smell to recognize each other. In most mammal species, a mother will not feed another mother's infant, even if it is the same age as her own. But she may be persuaded to accept an orphan if it is smeared with her own scent or that of her own young. Sheep raisers use that trick to get sheep mothers to raise orphaned lambs.

Sensing Danger

Have you ever noticed that a rabbit seems to twitch its nose almost all the time? That's because it uses its keen sense of smell to sense danger. A rabbit is prey to many animals—coyotes, foxes, weasels, hawks, owls, cats, dogs, and people. With so many kinds of predators, a rabbit must have a sharp sense of smell. Rabbits have a special device that allows them to smell effectively. Flaps of skin open and close over the nostrils, much as our blinking eyelids continually open and close over our eyes. Their action allows the rabbit to keep sniffing, bringing in new currents of air as its smell receptors recover from the last stimulation. As soon as the rabbit gets the scent of an intruder, it darts for cover to some hiding place.

Certain plants and insects have special chemical weapons to protect themselves from danger. These plants and insects are often brightly colored or marked with easy-to-recognize patterns. Tiger moths, monarch butterflies, and ladybugs all advertise their poisonous nature with brightly colored markings and distinct smells. Their bodies are covered with bad-tasting poisonous chemicals that will make a predator very ill or even kill it. Animals quickly learn that species with such patterns are not good to eat. Some frogs are covered with striking colors also designed to warn their enemies to stay away—or get a mouthful of poison. Some plants produce poisonous chemicals that are deadly to their predators. An unknowing caterpillar or snail that feeds on this plant will not get a second chance.

Fur seals give birth on island beaches after a long ocean migration, and then they must go down to the water periodically to get food. The individual smell helps to guide them back to their pups on the crowded beaches.

Many important food crops, including fruits and vegetables, depend on bees for fertilization. Bees might even have helped create various flowers in the world by spreading pollen among different plants.

Humans have created special chemicals that are used to detect dangerous gas leaks. For instance, tiny amounts of a highly odorous substance (similar to a skunk smell), added to odorless natural gas, make it possible to detect gas leaks. Researchers have also designed various materials containing specialized sensors that are sensitive to certain odor molecules and can detect gas leaks.

Attractive Food

Did you ever wonder why flowers smell so good? We aren't the only ones who like the sweet-smelling fragrance of a flower. Bees and butterflies are attracted to a flower's smell. A sweet smell is a sign that a flower has good-tasting nectar as well. Flowers have a reason for smelling so good—it's their way of asking for help. When a worker bee drinks up the nectar, she picks up pollen on her head, feet, and other body parts. In her travels, the bee continues to pick up new loads of pollen and spreads it from flower to flower. In this way she pollinates the flowers, which helps them grow and produce more plants.

Six
PERSONAL SMELLS

Although the human sense of smell is not as keen as a dog's, we are able to recognize many of the fine differences that make up people's individual smells. Helen Keller, who became blind and deaf at nineteen months of age, sharpened her sense of smell so she could become better connected with the world around her. She could recognize friends and visitors by the way they smelled, and she amazed them by greeting them by name. She said that just by smelling people she could tell the kind of work they did, from the telltale odors of wood, iron, paint, or medicines that clung to their skin and clothes. She could also tell—just by smell—if a person had come from the kitchen, the garden, or the sickroom.

The average person relies more on sight and sounds for information about the world and is rarely conscious of individual smells (unless they are unusually strong or "different"). And yet studies have shown that people are surprisingly good at identifying personal odors.

Family Smells

Is there such a thing as a "family smell"? Various studies have shown that indeed there is. Mothers can recognize the smell of their newborn infants after only ten minutes of exposure. In a series of tests, most of a group of mothers who had recently given birth were able to pick out an undershirt worn by their own baby from shirts worn by other infants in the nursery. Some of the mothers commented that the shirts smelled like other children in the family.

Another study involved a group of fifteen mothers with three- to eight-year-old children. The mothers were given T-shirts to wear for three nights in a row. Then a group of people were given the shirts to smell and asked to match up the mothers with their children. The scores were much better than those that would have been expected by mere guessing. But in an experiment matching T-shirts worn by husbands and wives, the shirt sniffers did not score as many correct matches. Such studies suggest that heredity plays a larger role than environment in determining people's individual smells.

A person's body odor can change according to mood. For instance, your body odor while you are stressed and upset smells different from when you are relaxed and happy. The chemicals in your body change when your mood changes.

Food also affects a person's personal smell. Some experts say that vegetarians smell different from people who eat meat. People who eat odorous foods like garlic and onions smell different from those who eat mostly bland foods. These odors come through the pores in the skin.

Researchers have found that once newborn infants have been nursed by their mothers, they can direct themselves to their own mother's smell thereafter. Infants can even tell the difference between their own mother and another nursing mother.

Those Embarrassing Body Odors

Have you ever walked past someone who smelled pretty stinky? All you wanted to do was to get away quick. People in the United States tend to associate strong body smells with dirt and disease. We learn at a very young age that our culture considers certain odors to be "stinky."

What turns a normal personal smell into "bad body odor"? Many body smells are associated with the sweat glands in the skin. These glands are found all over the body, but many of them are concentrated in certain areas, such as the armpits, the palms of the hands, the soles of the feet, and between the legs. Sweat glands on the palms produce a thin, watery sweat, which has very little odor, but the sweat from glands in the armpits and groin contains volatile odor chemicals. Smelly body odors occur because the areas with the sweat glands are warm and moist—a perfect breeding ground for bacteria. The bacteria feed on sweat chemicals and on the body's dead skin cells, which produce smelly by-products as the bacteria break them down.

Racial Smells

Studies have shown that different races have different characteristic smells. Some of these differences are due to variations in diet: People in India, for example, eat a lot of curry and spices, a diet that is reflected in their body odor. Racial differences also depend on hereditary traits. Asians tend to have very little body hair and few sweat glands to produce odor chemicals. Koreans, for instance, have little body odor even if they do not wash regularly; underarm odor is so rare among Japanese that they consider it an illness. Caucasians, on the other hand, have more body hair and plenty of sweat glands. Africans have even more sweat glands. People's unconscious reactions to others who "smell different" can contribute to distrust and intolerance.

Understanding what causes these emotional reactions can help us to behave more reasonably.

"Bad breath" is another common body odor problem. Many people consider bad breath so embarrassing that even close friends are afraid to tell you about it, and you will probably be annoyed or angry if someone does mention it "for your own good." Yet everyone gets bad breath from time to time.

Strong breath odors can be caused by not enough tooth brushing and flossing, leaving food particles between the teeth. The mixture of food and saliva provides nourishment for mouth bacteria, which produce a smelly odor. The odor is usually strongest just after you wake up in the morning ("morning mouth"). There is a reduced flow of saliva during sleep, and what is produced tends to lie in pools in the mouth rather than swishing around to provide a washing action, as it does when you are awake.

Because the smell receptors in the nose adapt quickly to constantly present odors, people are not usually conscious of their own body odors, even when others might consider them particularly foul. When you sniff your underarm to determine whether you are socially acceptable or need to wash, you are able to pick up some of the sweaty scent because the armpit area is normally covered. Exposing it gives you a blast of more concentrated odor, to which your smell receptors have not yet had a chance to adapt. The same thing happens when you check to see if you have bad breath. If you put your hand in front of your mouth and nose and breathe out, you can sniff your breath to detect any odor. The odor chemicals from your breath will bounce off your hand and be forced directly into the nose for detection.

Covering Up Body Odor

Americans are so sensitive to bad odors these days that TV and radio commercials constantly try to sell us products to make us smell good. These advertisements offer medicated soaps, mouthwashes, hair shampoos, underarm deodorants, and foot sprays—all promising to kill germs and keep us smelling fresh. What these products mostly do, though, is cover up the unpleasant odors.

The scent of lavender can help a person relax.

The perfume industry is big business in America. Perfume companies spend millions of dollars in advertising every year to sell the idea of smelling good. Perfumes can produce all kinds of reactions in people. Some people are attracted to the smell of perfumes, while others are turned off by them. Perfumes are very subjective. A particular perfume may have a pleasing odor to one person, while another person may find the same perfume repulsive. In addition, the same perfume smells different on different people. A perfume that smells great on you may smell horrible on your friend. That's because everyone inherits a kind of "odor print." A person's own molecules, the perfume's molecules, and those in other personal products, such as soap and shampoo, all affect the fragrance of a perfume. The amount of perfume also makes a difference. Most people react negatively to someone who has put on too much even of a good-smelling perfume.

Studies have shown that perfumes can affect a person's moods. For instance, citrus and wintergreen smells can make a person more alert. A geranium or honeysuckle scent can help a person fall asleep. These smelling effects are examples of **aromatherapy**—a method that uses fragrance to affect or change a person's mood or behavior. Researchers hope to incorporate aromatherapy into businesses. For instance, citrus smells can keep pilots awake in the cockpit. Certain fragrances may make store customers want to shop. Fragrances also have the potential to provide a happier, more pleasant environment for workers, which may increase their productivity.

49

Seven
ARTIFICIAL CHEMOSENSORS

Tupa Mbae, a native healer in Paraguay, had an amazing ability to diagnose people's illnesses by smelling their shirts or underwear. It is hard for people in our culture to imagine a doctor doing this, but, in fact, doctors over the centuries have routinely used their noses as a guide in diagnosing their patients' problems. Today's doctors may do it too, although they may not be fully conscious of the hints that odors provide.

Various diseases produce characteristic body or breath odors. Chemicals called ketones, produced in a person with diabetes, give the breath a fruity odor. Certain types of cancer have a foul odor. A fishy smell suggests that the patient may have a kidney problem. A musky odor can be an early warning of liver problems. People with diphtheria have a sickeningly sweet smell, plague victims smell like apples, typhoid fever patients have an odor like freshly baked bread, and yellow fever produces a "butcher shop" odor. Cyanide poisoning gives off an odor of bitter almonds, and arsenic poisoning gives the victim a garlic odor.

Scientists have been trying to develop a variety of devices that can diagnose illnesses using specialized smell and taste sensors. Artificial chemosensors can be made far more sensitive than our human senses of smell and taste; they can be used to test substances that humans would find unpleasant or dangerous, such as blood, urine, saliva, or breath.

Various kinds of "artificial noses" are also making their way into the medical field. These devices can detect illnesses by analyzing odor chemicals in a person's breath. Some researchers have developed a diagnostic breath test that detects a bacterium, *Helicobacter pylori,* that causes peptic ulcer disease, an inflammation in the lining of the stomach or part of the small intestine. This breath test is a simple, painless procedure, in which the patient drinks a nonradioactive solution and then exhales a series of breaths into a breath analyzer. The technique is much less invasive than getting blood tests and having a stomach biopsy. Researchers claim that the method gives fast and reliable results.

A group of scientists in London reports that they have designed a breath test to distinguish between viral and bacterial infections. Determining the difference between these two kinds of infections is very important.

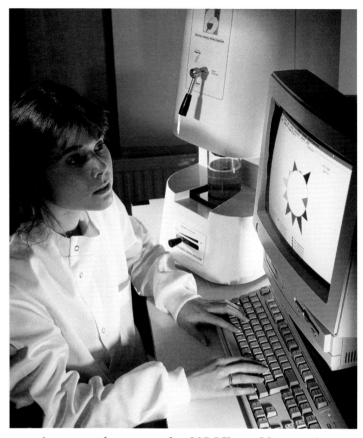

A researcher uses the NOSE, or Neotronics Olfactory Sensing Equipment, to analyze a glass of beer. The polar plot on the computer screen displays the various vapor components of the substance. NOSE technology can complement or even replace human quality control panels in the food and beverage industries.

Bacterial infections will respond to antibiotic drugs; viral infections, however, do not. Every year, doctors mistakenly prescribe antibiotics for patients with viral infections. People who take drugs unnecessarily may breed **drug-resistant** bacteria, and the medication will no longer be effective. These drug-resistant germs can spread through the population, causing illnesses that are difficult or impossible to treat. The new breath test could greatly reduce unnecessary prescriptions for antibiotics.

Kids Just Love to Spit

Oral biologist Rob Van Schie was working on a research project involving genetic screening for juvenile periodontal disease, an inherited form of gum disease in children, when he read a news report about a bombing investigation. FBI scientists were able to obtain a successful DNA analysis of dried saliva from a stamp used by the suspect. Van Schie thought this idea might be useful in his own work. He found that he could detect the same genetic information in saliva as he could in blood, and his young subjects enjoyed providing the "spit samples."

Artificial Tasters

Many things that doctors want to test for are not volatile. They are dissolved in body fluids. Therefore, testing typically involves collecting blood and urine samples. However, many people find these testing methods uncomfortable and invasive.

Can you imagine giving your doctor a "spit" sample instead of a blood sample? No needles, no invasion of privacy. Collecting saliva samples is less painful and safer than blood samples, and it eliminates the risk of infection. So far, saliva testing has been used to detect illegal drugs, alcohol, and periodontal disease and to monitor hormone levels. Studies have found, for example, that kids who are experiencing stress produce higher levels of a hormone called cortisol. In addition, studies on saliva testing showed that people with panic disorder had increased cortisol levels during panic attacks compared to when they were calm and relaxed.

In addition to their medical applications, artificial chemosensors are being used to monitor food for spoilage and test drinking water for harmful pollutants. Researchers are also developing implants for people who have lost their own chemical senses.

Artificial Nose

A police officer who suspects a person of being drunk can easily check by using a Breathalyzer. This chemical-sensing device analyzes the odor chemicals in a person's breath and determines the amount of alcohol that has been consumed. In many states, a device called an ignition interlock system is being used to keep drunk drivers off the road. To keep their driver's licenses, people convicted of driving while intoxicated must equip their cars or trucks with the device, which consists of a small breath analyzer connected to the vehicle's electrical system. Before starting up the engine, the person

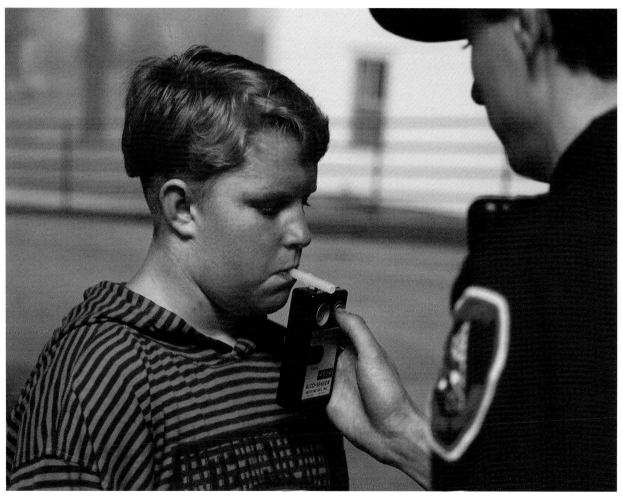

A police officer checks the odor chemicals in a boy's breath using a Breathalyzer, which determines the amount of alcohol he has consumed.

breathes into the mouthpiece of the device. A small display on the dashboard shows the amount of alcohol in the driver's breath. If it is more than 0.025, the car won't start. (The legal limits for intoxication are usually 0.08 or 0.10.) While driving, the driver must retake the test whenever the interlock system sounds a warning beep, to make sure he or she is not drinking while driving. Ignoring the beeping causes the system to record a violation. The breath alcohol detector in the interlock system is more sensitive than the Breathalyzer used by police; in fact, drivers are cautioned not to use mouthwash, breath spray, or cough syrup before taking the test.

Breath analyzers sensitive to alcohol have been used for many years. It was not until recently, however, that researchers designed other types of Breathalyzers and special "electronic noses" to be used in other ways as well.

The food and beverage industries have always used human testers to smell their products for quality and freshness. These people have a sharp sense of smell and can make sure that the product comes out the way it is supposed to. They can detect even slight variations in the production process and discard unacceptable products. The problem is that human sniffers do not perform consistently. Their noses may become less sensitive to particular smells over time, or they may be affected by colds, allergies, or other conditions. An electronic nose, however, is far more sensitive than a human's, and it can give fast, consistent results. It can also display a graphic record of the odor on a computer printout. Changes detected by electronic noses in the odor of corn, canola, and soybean oils can indicate when undesirable changes have occurred in their taste. The devices can tell the difference between vine-ripened tomatoes and those that were picked green, and between different-quality cuts of meat. They can not only identify particular varieties of rice but even indicate where they were grown! Electronic noses can also be a valuable tool in the perfume and deodorant industries, as well.

The Cyranose 320 contains a computer chip with an array of thirty-two sensors made of **polymers**, complex chemicals that expand or contract on contact with volatile substances. Each sensor responds to a different type of vapor. The chip is enclosed in a walkie-talkie-sized device equipped with a nozzle for collecting air samples. The changes in the polymers are translated into electrical signals that feed into a system of artificial neural networks—computer systems designed to work in a similar way to the biological neural networks that link the neurons in the brain. Just as our brain makes connections as we learn to identify new smells, the artificial networks are trained to distinguish certain odors from their characteristic chemical combinations. (With just thirty-two sensors, the Cyranose could theoretically be trained to recognize billions of different odors.) The electronic nose basically learns as it goes. The sensing system is instructed which odor samples are

A close-up of the detector head of an electronic nose shows that it consists of twelve conductive polymer sensors, which are complex chemicals that expand or contract on contact with volatile substances.

"good" or "bad," and neural connections are made. The network continues to adapt and change during its training period. After training, the electronic nose can check its memory bank to identify specific smells and determine if an odor sample is acceptable or not.

Electronic noses may ultimately replace the use of dogs in dangerous situations such as detecting gas leaks and locating land mines. There are now more than 100 million land mines buried in the ground of former battlefields in sixty-two countries in the

The disease diabetes
mellitus got its name
because the sugar that
passes out into the
patient's urine gives it
a sweet taste. (*Mellitus*
means "honey.")
None of today's
doctors would want
to taste a patient's
urine!

world, which are a danger to people and animals. The United States military uses metal detectors to find them, but small bits of metal and even certain types of soils can produce false alarms. Electronic land mine "sniffers" of several different types are now being developed. One takes samples in much the same way a dog sniffs the air, moving air samples back and forth over its "olfactory receptors." The vapors pass over a sensor array with thirty-two different polymers, each of which changes color when it comes in contact with particular chemicals. Odors are identified by a combination of the intensity of the colors and the rates at which the colors change.

Another land mine detector, about the size of a cigar box, uses a single polymer sensor containing a fluorescent dye. The sensor shines brightly when exposed to light, but if even a single molecule of explosive vapor attaches to it, the glow dims. This electronic nose can detect the explosive TNT in amounts as little as one hundred parts per quadrillion—the concentration that would result if an eyedropperful of the chemical were dissolved in an amount of liquid equal to the volume of twenty-five supertankers the size of the *Exxon-Valdez*. In field tests, the device was just as accurate as trained bomb-sniffing dogs.

A British electronics company has developed a security system that is keyed to a person's unique "smell print." This sensitive sensor system scans a person's hand to pick up his or her personal smell. The "smell print" is run through the computer databanks for positive identification. A correct match will allow entry in restricted areas. The manufacturers claim that the device will not be confused by food or environmental odors.

Blood tests have long been used to diagnose diabetes, an illness that is characterized by high levels of glucose (sugar) in the blood. People with diabetes need to monitor their glucose levels several times every single day by pricking their finger to get a drop of blood each time. Researchers have come up with a way that could make monitoring glucose levels hassle-free and a lot less painful. A glucose sensor is implanted just under the person's skin. Using a receiver that looks similar to a pager, the person can measure blood glucose levels at any time of the day without the trouble of frequent finger sticks.

Bionic Noses and Tongues

As researchers learn more about our chemical senses and design more effective artificial sensors, new possibilities are opening up. Perfume manufacturers are using new findings on sense receptor genes to design perfumes individually tailored to each user's ability to detect particular smells. Food manufacturers are studying recently discovered receptors for bitter and sweet tastes in efforts to make better-tasting medicines and foods.

The electronic noses built so far are still rather crude, containing only a few dozen sensors, compared with the millions in a human nose. But this research is just beginning. In the future, a "nose on a chip," implanted into the lining of the nasal cavity, may be used to help people who have lost their own sense of smell. Artificial taste buds may make eating pleasant again for people who have lost the ability to taste. It may even be possible to devise bionic noses and tongues capable of detecting odors and tastes that humans have never experienced before. Developments such as these, along with our ever expanding knowledge about the chemical senses and sensors, will enrich our lives with a wealth of new information about our world.

These odor fingerprints from an electronic nose represent four different odors: (clockwise from top left) rose petals, red wine, tobacco, and meat. The plots show the responses of the device's twelve sensors to the odors present—the circle indicates a zero response, triangles outside the circle indicate a positive response, and triangles inside the circle have a negative response.

GLOSSARY

allomones—chemicals produced by an animal that affect the behavior of animals of other species

amygdala—a structure in the brain involved in the formation of memories

aromatherapy—a method that uses fragrance to affect or change a person's mood or behavior

barbels—the whiskers of catfish

cerebral cortex—the thin, outermost layer of the brain where most of the activity in the brain takes place

cerebrum—the largest part of the brain, with which we think, remember, process sensory information, make decisions, and control the movements of the body

chemoreceptors—sensors sensitive to chemicals that come in contact with them

cilia—tiny olfactory hairs

cribriform plate—a thin portion of the bony skull that separates the nasal cavities and the brain

dissolve—to blend into a liquid, forming a uniform mixture (a solution)

drug-resistant—pertaining to germs that can no longer be killed by drugs that were formerly effective against them

flehmen response—a typical reaction of mammals to an interesting scent, in which the nose is wrinkled, the lips are curled, and air is drawn in to pass over the vomeronasal organ

glomeruli—nerve clusters inside the olfactory bulb, which send messages throughout the brain

glossopharyngeal nerve—a nerve found at the back of the tongue, involved in tasting

glutamine receptor—a protein on nerve and sensory cells that responds to glutamine, an amino acid (one of the building blocks of proteins)

gustation—the sense of taste

gustatory receptors—cells that react to taste chemicals

hippocampus—a structure in the brain involved in the formation of memories

hypothalamus—a structure deep inside the brain that contains centers controlling appetite, fear, anger, and pleasure

invertebrates—animals without a backbone or an internal skeleton

Jacobson's organ—two small pockets in the roof of the mouth that contain olfactory receptors; mostly found in reptiles

limbic system—part of the brain that is involved with emotions

lingual nerve—a major nerve found in front of the tongue, involved in tasting

medulla—medulla oblongata, the bottom part of the brain stem

molecules—smallest units of chemical compounds

monosodium glutamate (MSG)—a salt of glutamine used as a food seasoning

myelin sheath—fatty covering that surrounds nerve cells

nasal cavities, nasal passages—two tunnels that run from the nostrils to the upper part of the throat

nerve fiber—a long, thin, threadlike portion of a neuron

neuron—a nerve cell, specialized for carrying messages in the form of electrical signals

nostrils—two external openings in the nose, used for breathing and smelling

odorant-binding proteins (OBPs)—proteins with cup-shaped openings that hold onto incoming odor molecules and carry them up to the olfactory cells

olfaction—the sense of smell

olfactory areas—smell centers; the parts of the brain that control smelling

olfactory bulb—a tiny bulb-shaped structure found in the lower part of the brain just above the nasal cavity; it contains clusters of nerve cells (glomeruli) where different odors are sorted out

olfactory epithelium—a tiny, mucus-covered patch on the roof of each nasal cavity that contains millions of olfactory receptors

olfactory nerve—a thick cord of nerve cells that sends nerve signals from the nose to the brain, where they are translated into meaningful smells

olfactory pits—two small openings in the nose of a fish that take in odor molecules

olfactory receptors—nerve cells that react to odor chemicals

papillae—tiny bumps on the tongue that contain the taste buds

pheromones—chemicals produced by an animal that affect the behavior of other animals of the same species

polymer—a complex chemical compound made up of many small molecules joined together

primary olfactory neuron—the nerve cell running up from the olfactory epithelium in the nose to the olfactory bulb

proboscis—long, coiled beak found in insects

rhinencephalon—the "smell brain," consisting of the olfactory bulbs and the olfactory areas of the cerebral cortex

saliva—watery fluid in the mouth that is released by the salivary glands

sensors—specialized structures that gather information about the world by detecting various types of energy or chemicals and transmitting signals to the brain

sex attractant—a kind of pheromone that helps a male find his mate

tarsus (*plural* **tarsi**)—the last segment of an insect's leg

taste buds—structures on the surface of the tongue that contain taste receptors

taste receptors—chemical-sensitive cells found in the taste buds

thalamus—a small cluster of cells in the front of the brain stem that acts as a central switchboard to sort out and relay incoming information

umami—a savory or meaty taste, produced by the response of glutamine receptors on the surface of taste buds

vagus nerve—a nerve found at the throat and windpipe involved in tasting

vertebrates—animals with a backbone and an internal skeleton

volatile—turning into gases fairly easily

vomeronasal organ (VNO)—a structure in the nasal cavity of mammals that is used to analyze odor molecules, particularly those of pheromones

FURTHER READING

Barré, Michel. *Animal Senses.* Milwaukee: Gareth Stevens Publishing, 1998.

Cobb, Vicki. *How to Really Fool Yourself: Illusions for All Your Senses.* New York: John Wiley & Sons, 1999.

Hellman, Hal. *Beyond Your Senses: The New World of Sensors.* New York: Lodestar Books, 1997.

Hickman, Pamela. *Animal Senses: How Animals See, Hear, Taste, Smell, and Feel.* Buffalo: Kids Can Press Ltd., 1998.

Llamas, Andreu. *The Five Senses of the Animal World: Smell.* New York: Chelsea House Publishers, 1996.

Llamas, Andreu. *The Five Senses of the Animal World: Taste.* New York: Chelsea House Publishers, 1996.

Parker, Steve. *Look at Your Body: Senses.* Brookfield, CT: Copper Beech Books, 1997.

Santa Fe Writers Group. *Bizarre & Beautiful Noses.* Santa Fe: John Muir Publications, 1993.

Santa Fe Writers Group. *Bizarre & Beautiful Tongues.* Santa Fe: John Muir Publications, 1993.

Silverstein, Alvin and Virginia. *Smell, the Subtle Sense.* New York: Morrow, 1992.

Taylor, Helen. *You'd Never Believe It But...Flies Can Taste With Their Feet and Other Facts About Senses.* Brookfield, CT: Copper Beech Books, 1998.

Vroon, Piet. *Smell: The Secret Seducer.* New York: Farrar, Straus and Giroux, 1997.

INTERNET RESOURCES

tqjunior.thinkquest.org/3750/smell/smell.html
"Your Sense of Smell."

tqjunior.thinkquest.org/3750/taste/taste.html
"Your Sense of Taste."

www.4ffs.com/_vti_bin/shtml.exe/enhancer.html/map
"Flavor Enhancers."

www.hhmi.org/senses
"Seeing, Hearing, and Smelling the World: New Findings Help Scientists Make Sense of Our Senses," The Howard Hughes Medical Institute.

www.mayohealth.org/home?id=HQ01489
"Taste & Smell: Taste Buds Are Not Always to Blame," Health Oasis Mayo Clinic, July 1997.

www.time.com/time/magazine/articles/0,3266,40731,00
"Electronic Noses Sniff Out a Market or Two," by Unmesh Kher, March 2000.

INDEX